PODCAST

Learn how to stop babbling
& start podcasting like a pro

MIKE EIMAN

Podcast: Learn How to Stop Babbling & Start Podcasting Like a Pro

www.mikeeiman.com

ISBN: 9781521996225

CONTENTS

INTRODUCTION

Why Read This Book?

There are dozens of websites, videos and other resources about podcasting. They cover topics like which microphone to buy, which software to use, how to host your media files and getting started with iTunes.

But all the help stops once you sit down to record your show. Maybe you're the most interesting person in the world with a million interesting things to say. That won't stop you from freezing up and telling yourself, "I don't know what to say."

If you're reading this, you probably have some of the same questions I had when I started to learn about podcasting.

- What do I say when I put my face up to the microphone?
- What skills do I need to make a podcast?
- Should I write a script or just improvise?

You might get so caught up with questions that you never record your first episode.

The most overlooked component of recording a podcast tends to be in the planning stage. We all want to sit down in front of a microphone and just start talking. This can be so intimidating that you convince yourself that you can never be a podcaster.

Some professionals are very skilled at improv. The ability to talk without a script takes years of practice. Most professional programs are a mix of scripted and unscripted segments.

Listen to any of your favorite podcasts. Can you tell if the host is reading or ad-libbing? This is actually a fun exercise. It's amazing how much of a 30-minute or 60-minute show is planned in advance. Introductions, commercials and closing comments are almost always scripted.

Unless you're a veteran public speaker with a knack for ad-libbing, outlines and scripts are going to be your best friend for a while.

This book will walk you through the process – although there are many ways to do it – to plan and record your first podcast episode. After you've done it a few times, you might start to develop your own methods that best suit your strengths.

To practice these methods, you will need the following:

- A way to record yourself speaking (i.e. digital recorder or computer software)
- Word processing software with the ability to set margins.
- A quiet place to work

CHAPTER ONE

What To Know Before You Start

So you've got a great idea for a podcast. You bought a fancy microphone and a bunch of other stuff you read about online. Maybe you're paying a company like SoundCloud or Libsyn to host your media files.

Great. You've already spent $100 to $200 (or more if you got a really fancy microphone).

But you sit down in front of the microphone and press record – and now what? What are you supposed to say?

Maybe Google has the answer.

You search around but come up empty handed. The top search results for "how to podcast" are pretty useless unless you have a background in broadcast media. These sites offer microphone recommendations, recording tips and vague instructions like "write a script" or "make an outline."

This is like telling someone who wants to build a house that all they need is a hammer, nails and some building materials.

Whether you're building a podcast or a house, you need a blueprint and some basic skills. So before you buy a bunch of crap, you need to know what you're building.

What's your motivation?

Podcasts can serve a variety of purposes. They can be used to promote a person or a business. They can serve as a platform to share ideas, news or other information. Or they can be a great way for you and your buddies to immortalize some crazy conversations.

So what'll it be? Business or pleasure?

Either way, you will need a solid idea for your show. That includes having a general topic and overall format for the presentation.

Exercise #1

Maybe you dream of being a famous podcaster but you don't have any ideas. That's OK. For the purposes of this book, all you need is a topic that you're interested in. Maybe you're a news junkie or you enjoy talking about art, music or science.

Make a list of 10 things you like to talk about. If this takes less than five minutes, think of a few more. The point is to get beyond the obvious choices and tap into the creative part of your brain.

Put a star next to your top three ideas. If nothing jumps out at you, ask a friend to weigh in. Or repeat the exercise and exclude anything that was on your first list.

There. Now you have an idea to at least get you started.

If your podcast will be promoting a person or a business, you will probably want to spend more time in the planning phase. You'll need to think about how podcasting fits into your overall business plan and how you will attract an audience.

That's beyond the scope of this book. There are plenty of resources on business and marketing. But you need to keep those things in mind.

On the other hand, if you're just podcasting for fun, that stuff isn't really important. You might want to learn about it later. But "Five Dudes Talking in the Garage" probably doesn't warrant a detailed business strategy.

Who's your audience?

It's important to know who you're talking to when dealing with any form of mass communication. You wouldn't talk to your boss the same way you would talk to your significant other.

Here are some factors to consider about your typical listener:

- **Age**
- **Gender**
- **Educational background**
- **Income** (this is especially important if you will have commercials)
- **How many people do you expect to listen to your podcast?** This could vary based on your topic, target demographic and whether you expect to have an existing audience follow you from a blog or other platform.

You might have no idea about this stuff. Don't worry too much if you don't know. Just guess how big your audience might be. Will it be your mom and a few of your friends? Or can you reasonably expect to reach a few thousand people in a particular niche.

A final consideration will be how you will engage with your audience. Do you have a website? Do you need one? Is there a particular social media platform where you are more likely to reach your target listeners? You should try to set up these accounts in advance, as you will be directing people to use them when you start writing scripts and/or show outlines later in this book.

Length & frequency

Audio programs are typically divided into 15-minute units. This has held true since the days when families gathered around to "watch" the radio.

You have to decide in advance how long you want your podcast to be. If you're a beginner, a 15-minute program will be easier to wrap your head around. A show that's 30 minutes or longer will require more planning, production and showmanship. Longer programs typically include multiple segments, transitions, music cues and other features.

The length should be determined based on the topic and your audience's listening habits. Check out some of the popular podcasts in your niche.

Don't forget to consider how much content you

can reasonably expect to produce on a regular basis.

Along with your show length, you have to decide how often you will produce new episodes. Is this a daily podcast? Biweekly? Weekly?

If you're a lone wolf podcaster, it's probably unrealistic to produce a daily hour-long show with scripted segments, interviews and other original content. That level of work requires a production team to help with the writing, scheduling of guests and managing the technical aspects of the show.

The length and frequency boils down to two questions:

1. How much work am I capable of doing?
2. How much work am I willing to do?

Types of content

Cool. Now you know your motivation, you have a topic and you know your show's length and frequency. But what the heck are you supposed to talk about for 15 minutes? Thirty minutes? An hour?

Common types of content can be divided into a few major categories. Each of these will be indicated in some form when you start writing your script.

1. Information

If you're promoting a business or focusing on a specific topic, you will most likely focus on presenting information-based content. It could also be described as "how to do it."

Information can be based on formal research, interviews or even personal experience. The point is to provide the listener with some kind of take-away message. Maybe you have a web design business and you want to talk about common mistakes you see on the Internet. Or maybe you're talking to a public figure about their personal philosophy.

Lots of hosts fill their podcasts with funny or interesting stories. The host of a show about business might relay their own experience with a particular subject.

2. News

One of the most common forms of content is news. This can include reports about local, state, national or world events. News can be divided into any number of categories, but some of the biggies are:

- **Hard News** - politics, finance, crime, environment, etc.
- **Sports** - reports about various games, scores, play-by-play analysis
- **Entertainment** - TV, movies, celebrity gossip
- **Special Interests** - Health, science, food, technology

3. Music

There are a few different ways to use music as part of an audio program.

You might choose adopt the classic radio model of featuring music to help promote the artist. This comes with various legal requirements.

Another approach is to simply use original or licensed music (i.e. no one will sue you for using it) for intros, transitions and endings. This is probably your best bet. Music can add a lot of glitz and production value to your podcast. If you or a friend can compose music for the show, you have a leg up on the competition.

Music can also be used as a "bed," meaning it plays quietly in the background while someone is talking. This can add to the mood of whatever the speaker is talking about. Just make sure the feeling of the music matches the subject matter.

4. Commercials

Depending on your financial goals, you may need to have some commercials. Don't overdo it. A 30-minute show should not have 20 minutes of commercials.

Only advertise products and services that are relevant your audience. Most people will stop listening if you hit them over the head with too many commercials or products they're not interested in. Your listeners care more about your content than your ads. Both content and ads should provide value, even if only one of them pays your bills.

Segments

We've already established that audio programs are divided into 15-minute units. But that doesn't mean that all of your content will be split into 15-minute chunks. Each unit of time can be further subdivided into segments.

A segment is a piece of content that contributes to the overall structure of your podcast. Examples of segments could include:

Straight talk:
This is where a single host does all the talking. It could be fully scripted, improvised or follow an outline. Straight talk gets boring after a few minutes if you don't break it up with music or other segments.

Discussion:
You might have a show with multiple hosts. One

person sets up a topic and the others chime in to keep the conversation going. Another form of discussion involves inviting multiple guests to sit on a panel.

Interview:

An interview is usually a one-on-one Q&A or discussion. It might focus on a single topic or jump around.

Produced Content:

You don't have to rely on in-studio guests and interviews. If you have some portable recording gear, you can go out into the world to capture audio. Or maybe you have a long-distance acquaintance who wants to send in an MP3 of a segment they recorded. With either of these circumstances, you can drop the audio into your favorite editing software and make it part of your show. Just be sure you and your friends aren't using any copyrighted material without permission.

Now you have some ideas for how to divide your show. Here's a rough picture of what a 15-

minute show could look like divided into segments:

I. **Intro** (1 minute)
II. **Welcome/summary** (single speaker, 2 minutes)
III. **Interview** (host/guest, 10 minutes)
IV. **Call to action** (single speaker, 1 minute)
V. **Closing** (1 minute)

The times used above are only estimates. You might choose to jump right into the show and skip the intro, have two 5-minute interviews or give a solo talk for 10 minutes. The point of this is to get you thinking about time.

A 15-minute show will likely only have about 12 or 13 minutes of new content. You'll spend some time introducing yourself, your show and what you're going to talk about. Then you'll launch into your interview, discussion, feature, etc. for about 10 minutes.

You can end the show by telling people where they can find more about you or your guests (websites, blogs, Facebook, Twitter).

Once you understand basic structure, the idea of producing a 15-minute show doesn't sound that scary. The intro and closing will be pretty much the same for every episode. The welcome/summary and the call-to-action will follow the same format every episode.

Awesome. That means you're only on the hook for about 10 minutes of totally original content. If you're writing a script, that's about 10 pages of text with double spacing and really wide margins.

Exercise #2

Now it's your turn. Get a sheet of paper and write out the structure for your podcast. Try to limit yourself to something you could actually produce in a weekend. If you don't have access to any guests to interview, don't say you're going to have a 10-minute interview.

You may already have an intro and closing for your show. Great. Use the exact run times. Otherwise, assume 30 seconds to one minute for each.

Don't be afraid to have two or three segments. But keep in mind that extra segments need transitions – either narration or music cues – to avoid confusing the listener. Transitions can take extra time.

CHAPTER TWO

Planning Your First Episode

Now that you've decided what kind of show you want to produce, it's time to start getting your hands dirty.

For the purposes of this book, we're going to create a 15-minute weekly podcast. The process will about the same for a one-hour daily podcast. But the goal is for you arrive at a finished product, not to get bogged down trying to gather an hour of content every day.

In the previous chapter you learned that audio

programs are divided into 15-minute units. Those units can be further subdivided into segments, or bite sized pieces of content.

The average listener needs variety to sustain their attention. If you're hosting a political program, you can't read from the latest Senate subcommittee report verbatim for an hour. A minute might even be pushing your luck.

Unless you're telling a really interesting story or sharing some compelling information, most listeners will zone out after a few minutes of hearing a single speaker. They might last a little longer if you're interviewing someone or hosting a panel discussion.

Radio hosts have long relied on things like listener phone calls, weather reports and traffic updates to break up the monotony during a one or two hour broadcast.

Unfortunately, podcasting doesn't lend itself to weather and traffic updates. Few shows are released the same day they're recorded. No one cares on Friday about Wednesday's weather forecast.

So how the heck are you supposed to fill up your allotted time? Start at the beginning.

The intro

A simple 15-minute program might consist of an intro, welcome message, one or two short features, recap/call-to-action and a closing.

The intro and closing will likely be the same for every episode. The intro should include theme music, the title of your show and a brief description of what the show is about. You have to capture attention and set the stage for what's to come (i.e. branding).

A first-time listener will immediately know what to expect. Repeat listeners will wait in anticipation for the new episode to begin.

Grabbing Attention

The most important task of your intro is to grab people's attention. That means it not only has to sound cool, but it has to be appropriate for your topic and your target audience.

Your intro sets the mood for the podcast. If the intro is really loud and obnoxious, but your show is actually pretty laid back, you're setting yourself up for failure. Many podcasts rely on free loops or royalty-free music for the intro. This is fine if you're podcasting for fun.

The right music or sound effects will go a long way to grab your listeners and tell them who you are before anyone starts talking. The wrong music will, at best, kill time. At worst, it will put your listener in the absolute wrong state of mind and increase the chances they'll stop listening within the first few minutes.

Listen to some of your favorite podcasts. How do they handle this balancing act? Do they only use music, or is there a voiceover component as well?

Exercise #3

Find a comfortable place to sit. Grab a notebook and a pen. Now close your eyes (unless you think that's dumb) and try to hear the intro to your show.

Maybe it's a hard-rocking guitar riff and a gravel-voiced announcer saying, "You are listening to the (insert title here) where we take a deep dive into the nuts and bolts of (topic). And now your host, (your name here)." Then the music fades and you start telling everyone how great today's show is.

Maybe you hear a thumping electronic dance beat and an over-the-top voiceover saying, "This is the (your title) with (your name)!"

Your mileage may vary. But write down any ideas that come to mind. The alternative to this exercise is to choose the first piece of free music you can tolerate and try to make it work for an intro.

Who Are You & Why Do We Care?

What information does the audience need before you jump into the meat of your show? Maybe they visited your website and read your description before they downloaded your podcast in iTunes. But maybe they just liked your cover art.

Try to summarize in one or two sentences what your show is trying to accomplish. You can do this on the same piece of paper you used for Exercise #3.

What kind of value does your show offer to listeners? Is it tips and tricks for succeeding in a particular field? Or a unique spin on politics or celebrity gossip? Whatever it is, you need to state it here or in your welcoming narration (discussed later).

You might also name the show's host(s). Many shows do this in both the intro and the welcome message.

Keep in mind that audio is not like printed words. If a listener misses someone's name, they can't glance back to see what they missed. This is especially important if there are multiple hosts. Your listeners will eventually want to put a name to each voice. Each host should state their own name to reduce confusion.

Welcome To The Show

Assuming your intro did its job, people are still

listening at this point. Now you need to talk about what your listeners can expect from this episode.

If your intro didn't give a brief description of the show, now is the time to do it. If it did, you might decide to repeat it. Here is a silly example of a welcome message:

HOST:	Hello, and welcome to the Aerodynamic Kitten Podcast where you can hear new stories every week about the latest breakthroughs in feline aviation. My name is Bob Katz. I'm a certified feline aviation specialist and the publisher of "Cat Flight Magazine." Today we're going to be talking with award-winning author Kelly Boomer about her latest book, entitled "The First Cat in Space." It's really a great read. I highly recommend it. I first met Kelly at a conference back in 2008...

You get the idea. Expand on the "Who are you and why should we care?" question from earlier. In this case, the host establishes that he's an expert in his field. We also know that this is a weekly podcast that will share stories related to the topic.

Next, we find out what today's episode is about. The host introduces the guest and transitions into an anecdote about how he knows her.

This is just one way to set up the show. There is no right way. Just don't spend too much time introducing yourself every episode. Also, don't spend too much time telling people what you're going to be talking about.

There is nothing more frustrating than a host who is clearly stalling to fill airtime. If you don't get to the point – the part of your title and description that made someone click on it in the first place – your listeners will go elsewhere.

Don't overload the welcome message with advertisements. If you plan to use ads, try to only place one ad in the first few minutes of the show. Some shows feature an ad before the intro.

People want to hear your guest or the information you promised them in the title. The longer you make them wait, the more likely they will simply go elsewhere.

Transitions

After you finish your welcome speech, it's tempting to launch right into the next segment. Remember that unlike printed words, audio can't convey paragraph breaks or subheadings. You have to use some combination of words, music and sound effects to let people know you're moving on.

Sometimes the host will say something like, "And now let's jump into my interview with (guest's name)."

This could be followed by a short jingle or a sound effect to signify the transition from your solo narration to a dialogue or some other feature.

Recap and call to action

Most shows are "bookended" by the intro/welcome at the beginning, and a recap/closing at the end.

The recap will summarize key points and tell listeners where they can find more information about your topic or guest. This is the time to mention your website, Facebook, Twitter, etc.

Don't list too many things. If your listeners are driving to work or out for a morning run, they aren't going to visit all of your sites right now. And they probably won't remember to do it later.

At this point, your outro music might start playing. The outro can have additional narration or you can keep talking until just before it ends.

Here is an example script:

HOST: A big thanks to Kelly Boomer for taking time out of her busy schedule to join us. For more about Kelly and her new book,

```
visit W-W-W dot "Boomer Space
Cats" dot com.

If you enjoyed this episode of
the Aerodynamic Kitten Podcast
- please subscribe and leave a
review in iTunes. Check out
"Cat Flight Magazine" at W-W-W
dot Cat Flight Mag dot com. I'm
Bob Katz. Thanks for listening.
```

Collecting material

So you have some idea about how to start and end a show. Great. But what goes in the middle?

Let's say you're planning a 15-minute show with an interview and a news segment. For simplicity we'll assume your intro, opening narration and closing will take a combined total of five minutes.

Wow. Ten minutes for two segments? How do we pull that off? The answer is organization.

If you only have five minutes for an interview,

you have a couple of choices. You could ask lots of questions and edit it down. That's ok if you don't mind wasting time. Or you can prepare a few well-researched questions.

Do some homework before you start writing questions, working on scripts or hashing out an outline. Gather up any notes, press releases and other information you plan to cover.

Obviously, podcasting doesn't have a time limit like terrestrial radio. Your interview can be as long as it needs to be. The point is to be consistent. Imagine if your favorite TV show was an hour sometimes, but other times, without warning, it was three hours long.

You might have an hour to spare. Those extra two hours could totally mess up your routine. What if the show shrunk to 15 minutes?

People build routines around content, or choose content to fit their routines.

Someone with a 10-minute commute to work will have different listening habits than someone with a two-hour commute. And both of them will differ from someone who listens to podcasts in their office or at the gym.

Make sure you have enough material to fit the show length you've chosen. But don't be afraid to start writing if you're unsure. The only way to improve your sense of time is to practice.

CHAPTER THREE

Writing Your Podcast

There are two ways to organize a podcast: write a script or use an outline.

One method isn't necessarily better than the other. Some tasks will be better executed using a detailed script, while others will benefit from a more relaxed ad-lib style that hits on a few bullet points.

The following section will help you decide which system will work best for you and the type of podcast you're planning to make.

To script, or not to script?

Scripts are great for organizing all of your material in one place. If you format your pages properly, your script will have a runtime equal to about one minute per page (i.e. 15-page script for a 15-minute show). You can also consider the best way to explain complex information.

If you're a producer, scripts also afford you the opportunity to approve or edit material before it's recorded.

Outlines are better suited to ad-lib segments, interviews and group discussions. It can be freeing to stick to a few bullet points, but otherwise participate in a natural conversation. Also, speakers who are better ad-lib performers than readers can avoid sounding like robots.

That said, outlines don't offer the same accurate time estimates like a script. You might decide that you have five minutes for a particular item, but you need to watch the clock intently to avoid going over or under your time limit.

An outline also refers to other books, notes and

source material you plan to use. But it's up to you to keep everything organized. If the third section of your outline refers to a recent newspaper article, you need to have the article or your notes at your fingertips. Otherwise you'll stumble when you get to that item.

Whether you choose to use a script, outline or a combination of the two, you will need to weigh the pros and cons of each method. If you're planning a news program, you might be able to get by with a script for the whole show. An interview-based show may only need scripting for the intro, call to action and maybe some commercials.

Here are a few pros and cons to help you decide what's best for your needs:

Scripting

The Good:

- A written script ensures the program will cover all desired material
- With correct formatting, scripts offer accurate runtime estimates (1 minute per

page)
- Accurately conveys facts, figures and other information
- Written materials allow for better oversight prior to recording

The Bad:
- Can feel stiff, especially in the hands of an inexperienced reader
- Not practical for segments with multiple speakers, interviews, etc.
- Writing out longer segments can be quite time consuming
- You might get caught up trying to write the "perfect" script and never record anything

Outlining

The Good:
- Ensures ad-lib presentations will cover specific topics
- Allows for more natural discussion, especially during interviews and group talks
- Items can more easily be taken out of order if the segment doesn't go as

planned
- Better suited for speakers who are skilled at ad-lib speaking

The Bad:
- Requires reader to decide in real time how to best convey information
- The host has to keep a close eye on the clock to avoid going overtime
- Outlines refer to source materials, but rely on the host to organize those documents
- Requires memorization or ad-lib of material that might be easier to script

Write like you talk

Writing a script for a podcast or radio program is different than other styles of writing. Literary and academic writing are primarily visual. The sentence structure and punctuation provides visual cues to help the reader understand what's being said. Those cues don't exist in verbal communication.

If you want to convey information verbally, you

have to write the way you talk. Your script should be "conversational." That means it won't look very pretty on paper. But at least you won't sound like a weirdo when you read it out loud.

Talking on paper

The style of writing that's used for broadcast media is often described as "talking on paper." The style we learn in school is more like "please, give me a good grade."

Imagine you're creating a podcast about nutrition. If you wanted to write an academic paper about the benefits of whole grains versus white flour, you might include lots of facts, figures and statistics.

Here is an example of a sentence for that type of writing:

> Research conducted by the University of Antarctica shows that consumption of whole grains as part of a balanced diet contributes greatly to

> overall health and wellbeing compared with equivalent consumption of refined white flour.

That's all gibberish. But you've probably read articles that are written that way. It's hard to read and even harder to listen to. How would you explain that sentence to a friend while you're sitting in the living room eating pizza?

It might sound more like this:

> There's a new university study that says whole grains are healthier than white flour.

Wasn't that better? And if your friend is interested in what you said, he might ask some follow-up questions. Which university? How did they reach that conclusion?

The point is that a spoken script should function like a conversation. Few people talk like we're taught to write in school. Think about the last time someone asked how your day was. Did your response involve an introduction, supporting paragraphs and a closing statement?

If you only have a few minutes to talk with someone, you don't tell them everything you know. Tell them a few facts as clearly as you can. Repeat information as necessary.

Consider the following exercise:

Exercise #4

Write a paragraph or two about what you did today. If you haven't done anything yet, write about yesterday. Include as many or as few details as you deem appropriate.

Now read your paragraph out loud. Imagine sitting across from a close friend or your significant other. Would you actually use these words to describe your day? Odds are that you would use shorter sentences, and perhaps ignore some grammatical rules.

Go back and rewrite your paragraph so that it sounds more like you're talking to your friend. If your first attempt already sounds perfect, great. The following sections will help you refine your skills.

How you talk

The most important aspect of speech is to clearly convey information. Some people are better at this than others. You probably know (or work for) a few people who can talk endlessly without saying anything.

Others seem to reach out and touch you with just a few words. We share their inspirational quotes on Facebook and Twitter. While you may not be as quotable as Thomas Jefferson, there are a few ways to make your speech clearer and more effective.

A word about sentences

This may feel degrading for a seasoned writer. But the truth is that you don't talk the way you write. One of the biggest differences is your sentences. Literary sentences tend to be longer and more complicated. Speech should consist of short sentences and simple words.

A simple sentence has a subject (the person or thing performing an action) and a verb (the action) and a complete thought. For example:

Bob walked to the store.

There's really only one way to interpret that sentence. It's pretty clear who (Bob) did what (walked) and why (to get to the store). Simple sentences are extremely effective and are ideal for broadcast communications.

You can convey more information using a compound sentence, which consists of two simple sentences joined by a coordinating conjunction (and, or, nor, but, yet, so). For example:

Bob walked to the store, but he forgot to bring his wallet.

A complex sentence is a simple sentence and one or more dependent clauses joined by a subordinating conjunction (when, because, although, while, after). A dependent clause is a phrase that can't stand alone as a sentence. You can probably tell from the explanation that this type of sentence might be harder to follow. For example:

Bob walked to the store because he needed to buy bread.

Or...

Because he needed to buy bread, Bob walked to the store.

KEEP IT SIMPLE

You can usually simplify compound and complex sentences. Sometimes it helps. Other times it can sound choppy and unnatural. One of our previous examples could be rewritten as:

Bob walked to the store. He needed to buy bread.

For improved clarity, you should also avoid relative clauses. These begin with relative pronouns or adverbs like "who," "which" or "where." A relative clause helps to break up longer sentences.

Bob, who was running dangerously low on coffee beans, walked to the store.

It works visually, but can become tedious for a listener. Notice how many words separate the subject (Bob) from the verb. It's easy to lose track of who we're talking about. This type of sentence should typically be broken into two simple sentences:

Bob walked to the store. He was running dangerously low on coffee beans.

OTHER TIPS AND TRICKS

Now that you understand how to write shorter, simpler sentences, there are a few ways to make them sound even more like natural speech.

Sentence Fragments

People don't always speak in complete

sentences. Sentence fragments work fine in the context of a larger discussion. Consider the question, "Where's Bob?" You might say, "At the store." Your favorite word processor would put a green squiggly line under it. It's wrong. But that's how we talk.

Parenthetical Statements

Speech often includes throwaway phrases at the beginning of a thought. These include "You know," "You see," "I mean," and "Of course."

Contractions

Formal writing styles tend to discourage the use of contractions (words like "can't," "won't," "there's"). Writing for broadcast is different. Instead of saying "I am happy," say, "I'm happy."

Emphasis through repetition

Printed words allow you to go back if you missed someone's name or lost track of what's going on. Don't be afraid to repeat key names, words and phrases. You might be tempted to replace names with pronouns. Too many pronouns require the listener to remember too many things and subconsciously replace "he" with "Bob" every time they hear it.

Note: These are just suggestions. Always remember your goal is to speak like you would to your friend in their living room. If your natural speech doesn't include some of these techniques, don't try to force them. Above all, listen to how people talk.

Chapter Four

Down To Brass Tacks

It's time to start writing your show. There are lots of ways to approach this. We're going to cover a nuts-and-bolts approach to writing your first script.

By the time you're finished, you may decide that you never want to record another fully scripted show again. Or you might wish someone had told you about this stuff sooner.

Whatever the case may be, it's good to have some foundational skills in writing and producing material for your podcast. You should have a basic understanding of how to set up your word processor for script writing and how to tackle the writing process.

Formatting

There are several ways to format an audio script. This book covers one style that is simple and effective. But the best way is whatever works best for you.

An audio script serves a very specific purpose. It needs to convey a message and be easy to read, both verbally and visually. It will have wide margins, big line spacing and visual cues to help with pronunciation, emphasis and emotion.

You could keep everything set to the default positions. That will only make things harder on yourself.

Margins

The body of your script needs to be formatted

into a fairly narrow column. One way to do this is to set the left and right margins to 1.25 inches. Move the "hanging" indent over another 2 inches. This allows you to write the speaker's name all the way to the left and push the dialogue into a column on the right.

Line Spacing

Double- or triple-space your script. This serves two purposes. It makes the lines easier to read, and it gives you room to write notes about pronunciation, emphasis and emotion.

Fonts

Use a font like Courier or some other fixed-width, typewriter-style. The most important aspect of your font choice is how easy it is to read.

Header/Footer

Include right-justified page numbers in the header, or center them in the footer. This is particularly useful if you plan to read your scripts from paper. Your pages will inevitably get out of order. NEVER STAPLE YOUR SCRIPT

TOGETHER.

Orphaned Sentences

The last thing you want is to be in the middle of reading a sentence and have to turn the page. If your word processor lacks a setting to handle this automatically, you need to go through your script and manually add returns to prevent unwanted page breaks.

Page one

The first page of your script should be your cover page. Cover pages are useful for quickly identifying a particular script. They also make your work look more professional, like you know what you're doing.

This will include basic information like the show title, episode number and who wrote the script. If you're working with other writers and will be editing each other's work, be sure to include a date or revision number in the header. This will ensure that everyone has the most recent draft.

You can add other information if necessary, but a typical cover page looks something like this:

```
                                        8/1/2017




           EXAMPLE PODCAST, EPISODE 1

                  Written By

                  Jane Smith
```

Writing your intro & outro

If you're a total beginner, you might want to use the same pre-recorded intro for every episode. A more experienced podcaster may decide to tailor the intro for each script.

There will be three main types of audio cues in your script: music, sound effects and dialogue. Each cue is labeled in capital letters on the left side of the page. The labels are followed by a colon and a tab 2 inches from the margin.

Music and sound effects cues are written in all caps, with bold and underlined text. This helps you avoid mistaking them for dialogue.

Here is an example intro script:

MUSIC: Theme song plays under announcer

ANNCR: You're listening to the EXAMPLE PODCAST. Every week we're gonna show you the best ways to make your podcast shine. I don't care how experienced you are, there's always room for learning.

MUSIC: FADE OUT

In general, your outro should be a call to action. It will ask listeners to visit your website, follow you on social media, subscribe to your show or leave a review in iTunes.

Exercise #5

Now it's your turn. Write an intro and an outro for your first episode. Be sure to mention who you are, what the show is about and why your listeners should care. After you finish, refer back to the sections on sentence structure and writing for speech.

Now read the exercise aloud. Record yourself speaking if you can. Does it sound like you're speaking or reading? If it sounds too stiff, your writing is too literary. Try eliminating some compound or complex sentences. Use contractions, sentence fragments and parenthetical phrases.

CHAPTER FIVE

The Main Program

A book can only give you so much guidance on writing the body of your show. But if you've been completing the exercises up to this point, you should have some idea of where to start. You should have an intro, outro and a list of segments.

Let's say you want to produce a 15-minute show. If your intro and outro take up about 2 minutes, you will need to write about 12 pages. That sounds like a lot until you remember that about one third of each page is white space. Plus, you're double spacing between lines.

The simplest way to tackle this much writing is to break it down into smaller chunks or segments. Start out by giving an overview of what the audience should take away from this episode. That could be as simple as:

HOST: Welcome to the Chees-a-reeno business podcast. Today we're talking about five ways to sell more stuff from your online store. I think this is something every small business owner struggles with. Maybe you've got a few sales. Maybe you've got a seven-figure business. But how can you push it to the next level? How do you reach your audience? How do you even get an audience?

The first thing...

If you're going to discuss five ways to improve online sales, you already have something of an outline. Devote a page or two of your script to each one and you pretty much have a show. If you can write more, or interview an expert on some of the methods, you might have a half-hour or hour-long show.

An outline should include a brief description of each component of your show, along with an estimated runtime. This document can be as precise as you need it to be. Unlike radio, there's no real downside of running over or under by a couple minutes. A podcast can't preempt the next show on the schedule.

Outline Of a 15-Minute Program

This is a sample of how your show might look in outline form:

Intro music / Narration	*(1 min)*
Overview	*(1 min)*
Five ways to increase your sales	
1. Define your audience	*(2 min)*
2. Engage on social media	*(2 min)*
3. Build your email list	*(2 min)*
4. Promotions	*(2 min)*
5. Paid advertising	*(2 min)*
Recap and call to action	*(2 min)*
Outro	*(1 min)*
Total	(15 min)

This example is not intended suggest that a list-style structure is the way to go. It's just an easy way to think about structuring your show. Your outline could consist of several loosely connected topics or break one major subject into bite-sized pieces.

Depending on your thinking style, you might do most of the outlining in your head. In that case you could write "How to increase your sales" and give yourself 10 minutes for that subject.

If you plan to record a one-on-one interview or a group discussion, you can either decide the length in advance or build the show around the interview. The outline for that type of show would look something like this:

Intro music / Narration	*(1 min)*
Overview	*(1 min)*
Interview	*(10 min)*
Recap and call to action	*(2 min)*
Outro	(1 min)
Total	(15 min)

A bit of style

Writing for audio requires attention to detail. You don't want stumble over your words. Is that an acronym or someone's name? Does that say that 301, or 30.1?

Pronunciation is one of the most important aspects of this writing style. There's no standard for how to do it. You just have to find what works for you. That said, there are a few tips to get you started.

Acronyms & Abbreviations

It would be embarrassing to introduce the CEO of a company as the "keeyo." You'd sound foolish discussing a high-profile Fibi investigation when you mean to say FBI.

To avoid these kinds of problems, write out abbreviations in all capital letters separated by dashes. Web addresses should even have the periods and slashes written as "dot" and "slash."

Proper Names

You won't always be talking about Jane Smith

from Los Angeles. That would be too easy. So what happens when you have to introduce Gurvinder Senghal from Schenectady, New York? You will want to write the names phonetically in parentheses, with each syllable separated by a dash. Put emphasized syllables in all caps.

Assuming you had trouble saying his first name, last name and city, our friend from earlier might be written as: Gur-VIN-der Sen-GALL from Skuh-NEK-tuh-dee, New York.

Numbers

In the previous example, you'll notice Fortune 500 is written out in words instead of digits. That's to avoid any confusion. Imagine trying to say 4,333,735,001. It's almost impossible to say it right without thinking about it. Instead, write it out as "four billion, three-hundred thirty-three million, seven-hundred thirty-five thousand, and one."

On a related note, audio is not great for communicating lots of figures or statistics. Assuming that big number we just wrote out is really important to your talk, you might just shorten it to "about four billion" or "about four point three billion.

Example

Let's say you need to introduce a guest named Jane Smith. She's the CEO of a Fortune 500 company called Fake Company. She has a special offer available for your listeners at www.fakecompany.org/jane. Also, her name isn't pronounced the way it looks because her parents were crazy or something.

HOST: We've got a great guest joining us today. Jane (JAY-nee) Smith (Smitt) is the C-E-O of Fake Company dot org. It's one of the fastest-growing Fortune Five-Hundred companies.

For a limited time, JAY-nee is giving our listeners a special fifteen percent discount.

Just visit W-W-W dot Fake Company dot org, slash Jane. That's J-A-N-E.

Pronunciations can be as exact or approximate as you need. Someone with a background in linguistics might prefer to write proper names using the International Phonetic Alphabet (IPA). Most writers will want to write whatever keeps them from stumbling or mispronouncing the name. Try writing it one way and then read the section out loud. If you got to the name and messed up, try writing it another way.

More tips on writing style

It's not enough just to write in a conversational manner and pronounce things correctly. You also have to present information more succinctly. Things like proper names, jargon words and numbers can quickly become confusing for the listener.

This is where writing for audio is different from regular conversation. If you're talking to your friend in her living room and you use an unfamiliar word, your friend can say, "Wait, what did you just say?"

Podcast listeners don't have that luxury. You have to take care not to leave anyone in the dust. Here are a few methods to improve the clarity of your message:

Names, Places And Other Keywords

Let's say you're commenting on a news event that involves the CIA selling Patriot missiles to rebels in Wharzbadistan (a fictional country). Rather than repeat yourself, you might be tempted to say "the agency" instead of "CIA" or refer to Wharzbadistan as "the country" after the first reference. Don't be afraid to repeat keywords. It might sound weird, but it will reduce confusion for listeners who missed it the first time and don't want to rewind.

Difficult Words/Concepts

Does your audience know this word? Are they familiar with a concept? If you're not sure, explain it or find a way to leave it out. A confusing word or concept could distract your listeners and make them miss whatever comes after it. Maybe they'll stop listening entirely. "This show is too confusing. Let me find another show on this topic."

Abbreviations And Acronyms

Just like a difficult word, don't assume your audience knows what an abbreviation or acronym means. It's safe to assume that most Americans will understand FBI, CIA and the DMV without further explanation. But what if you're talking to an entrepreneur about MVP? Are we talking about a "Most Valuable Player" or "Minimum Viable Product"? Would a first-time listener know which one?

Numbers And Figures

Avoid using lots of numbers. Most people can only retain two or three numbers in the context of a conversation. If you absolutely have to share some statistics or figures:

- Stick to two or three key points.
- Avoid percentages. Say "half" instead of "50 percent."
- Use visual comparisons whenever possible. If you're describing something that's about 150,000 square feet, say it's about the size

of two football fields.

- Round large numbers. Unless the exact figure is crucial, it's better to say about 200 people attended the event. The company is valued at about $200 billion. Numbers larger than 1 million should be rounded to the nearest hundred thousand. For example, $1,578,000 would become "about $1.6 million."

Quotes

Be sure to clearly mark direct quotes in your script. Preface them by saying "quote." If the end of the quote isn't readily apparent, say "end of quote." You might prefer to use indirect speech like, "Smith says the company is on track for its most profitable quarter ever."

Visuals

Describe visuals whenever possible. Radio is often referred to as the "theater of the mind." Don't go overboard. It might be enough to say that someone lives in a simple two-bedroom house in a quiet middle-class neighborhood.

Unless it's crucial to your script, don't feel obligated to describe the trim, how many windows there are or what kinds of plants are growing in the front yard.

CHAPTER SIX

Delivering The Goods

Having a well-planned podcast and a perfect script doesn't guarantee success. You still have to deliver the goods, which means giving a good performance.

Some people are natural performers. Others have to work at it like any other skill.

This chapter will cover three aspects of speech to help you improve your performance. These include pacing, articulation, and emotion.

You can't get good at anything just by reading about it. Listen to recordings of yourself and be critical. Ask a trusted friend for their opinion.

Pacing

Pacing is a good gauge of how well people can understand you. Words start to run together when you talk too fast. Slow talkers are tedious to listen to. If you're using the scripting format described earlier, you should be reading about one page per minute.

You can check your pace by multiplying the number of lines you can read in a minute by the average number of words per line (which should be about six words). This will give you the number of words per minute (WPM).

Once you've written the first draft of your script, time yourself as you read it aloud. You will need a timer or some kind of stopwatch app. Set the timer for one minute and read aloud until the alarm sounds. Count how many lines you read.

Our format allows for about six words per line

and about 24 lines per page. That's an average of 144 words per page. If you took exactly one minute to read a page, you would have a pace of 144 words per minute.

Most English speakers talk at about 100 to 150 WPM. This is a good rule of thumb.

Knowing your natural pace is very useful. You can use your WPM to:

- Calculate the runtime of your script (word count ÷ WPM)
- Help you adjust the margins so each page is about a minute
- Know whether your natural speech is too slow, or too fast

You might naturally talk slower or faster. Each page could include lengthy audio clips or music cues that might be several minutes long but use just one line of script.

Articulation

Articulation is a double-edged sword. Too much makes you sound like a robot. Not enough makes you impossible to understand.

Poor articulation is often a symptom of talking too fast. If you slur or stammer a lot, the first step is simply to slow down. Let's use a classic tongue twister as an example:

> Peter Piper picked a peck of pickled peppers.
>
> A peck of pickled peppers Peter Piper picked.
>
> If Peter Piper picked a peck of pickled peppers,
>
> Where's the peck of pickled peppers Peter Piper picked?

Try to read the example aloud at your normal speaking pace. If you stumbled, you were probably rushing. Read the example again, this time visualizing each word in your head as you say it. This will force you to slow down since it adds an extra step between seeing the word and saying it.

Another technique to help with articulation is to break sentences into smaller pieces. This is useful if you keep stumbling over certain parts of your script. If you can, rewrite the sentences so they're easier to speak. Hopefully your writing style isn't as tricky as Peter Piper.

If there's no way to rewrite it, or if you're reading a commercial exactly as your sponsor requested, draw lines between phrases:

```
Peter Piper / picked a peck /
of pickled peppers.

A peck / of pickled peppers /
Peter Piper picked.

If Peter Piper / picked a peck
/ of pickled peppers,

Where's the peck / of pickled
peppers / Peter Piper picked?
```

Feeling

Musicians use dynamics and pitch to create different moods. A violinist playing a series of notes quietly and with ease won't convey the same feeling as a wailing rock guitar solo. Good music is full of emotion. It tells a story without words.

Your voice should do the same thing. For instance, you wouldn't use the same tone of voice to describe a horrific car accident as you would to talk about your new puppy. This concept is critical to an audio podcast.

Your audience can't see your face. That means you have to convey all of your feelings vocally. How you do this is totally personal. It's what will set you apart from other podcasters.

Although no one can see you, your face and physicality can be key components to expressing emotion. Consider the following sentence:

> *The president sent his condolences to the soldier's widow Tuesday night, saying, "We owe your husband a great debt for his service to our country."*

Read the sentence aloud. Read it again in a monotone voice. You should sound like an emotionless robot. Now sit up straight, smile really big and try reading it again. This time you should sound bright and energetic, which is totally inappropriate for this somber message.

Now try furrowing your brow and lowering your head slightly. Read the sentence again. How did you feel? If the tone wasn't quite right, try adjusting your facial expression and posture until you feel like you've captured the proper emotion.

Some newscasters mark their scripts with smiley faces, frowny faces and other symbols to indicate what kind of feeling they need to convey. This makes it easier to transition from a happy subject to a sad one, or vice versa, without sounding like a psychopath.

CHAPTER SEVEN

Outlining & Ad-Lib

Ad-libbing sounds easy: You just make it up as you go.

Many podcasts feature hosts who essentially talk about nothing for 20 or 30 minutes. It might be fun for the host, but this shows total disregard for anyone who attempts to listen to their show.

The goal of a good podcast is not to simply fill time with idle speech. You have to provide your audience with some kind of value. Unless you're a seasoned public speaker, you will probably fail if you try to "wing it" without an outline.

An outline is basically a list of points you want to cover during your program. It might refer to research and personal notes that you will refer to for information. Outlines have less information than a script, but they ensure that your babbling will follow some kind of structure. Even the best outline won't improve your ad-libbing skills. That takes practice.

Blind leading the blind

How do you know if you stink at improvising? If you have little or no experience, you can almost be certain you're not doing very well. The same goes for talking about a subject you've done little or no research about.

Imagine if someone asked you to give a presentation about dinosaurs. Would you do some research first? Or would you show up and wing it? After all, you've seen "Jurassic Park" like 50 times. T-rex, velociraptor, lawyer getting eaten on the toilet. That's 15 minutes of material right there. What else do you need to know?

Tackling your dinosaur presentation without research or an outline will lead to one of two problems: talking too much or not enough. Even if you have a basic outline in your head, you might forget key points or spend too much time on minor points.

If you want to teach others about a subject, you have to become more knowledgeable and organized than your audience.

Research

Research sounds scary. In reality, it's as simple as going to Google, typing in your topic and skimming through the top results (assuming you're not planning to take credit for copyright-ed material). If there is a government agency that compiles facts or statistics about your topic, you should definitely take advantage, as that information is likely in the public domain.

For example, if we wanted to do some general

research about dinosaurs, we could add ".gov" to our search to see if there is any public domain information available.

At the time of this writing, there is a link to the U.S. Geological Survey website with an article called "Dinosaurs: Facts and Fiction." The article appears to be old and outdated, but is still useful as the basis for an outline.

Dinosaurs Outline

- **When did dinosaurs first appear?**
    - 230 million years ago in Argentina/Brazil
    - Most primitive type is the Eoraptor
    - Advanced skeletal features suggest older dinosaurs may be found.
- **Where did dinosaurs live?**
    - Scientists believe they lived on all five continents.
    - During the Triassic Period (230 million years ago), the continents were arranged into a supercontinent called Pangaea.
    - The continents drifted apart during the 165-million-year existence of dinosaurs.
    - This process is called "plate tectonics."
    - Caused by volcanoes, earthquakes, mountain building and sea-floor spreading
    - This process still affects modern Earth.
- **Were humans around back then?**
    - No. Humans didn't appear until about 65 million years after dinosaurs.
    - Small, shrew-sized mammals did coexist with dinosaurs.
    - Some scientist believe modern birds are direct descendants of dinosaurs

---

Source: http://pubs.usgs.gov/gip/dinosaurs

We could flesh out this outline more, but this book would turn into a book about dinosaurs instead of one about podcasting. Based on the three main points above, you should be able to give a brief talk about dinosaurs. You can ad-lib other ideas and refer back to your outline if you veer off course or run out of steam.

Outlining a group discussion

If your podcast has multiple hosts or includes a panel of guests, you can still benefit from having an outline.

Ideally, you can sit down with the group beforehand and have a brainstorming session. What is the main focus of this episode? What points do we want to make sure we cover?

Brainstorming right before you record also helps loosen people up and get them focused on the topic at hand. To encourage free discussion, you should only allow one person to have a copy of the written outline. This person will be responsible to jump in and refocus the group if the session veers off course or if you're running out of time to cover all of the main points.

The major advantage of a group is that it can discover new ideas on the fly. But if you don't have a starting point, it could take half an episode to discover anything remotely interesting. You've probably listened to some podcasts like this. This lack of preparation is painfully obvious and often discourages listeners from coming back.

Easy interviews

Interviews are deceptively simple. Most beginners think all they need a list of awesome questions and the rest will take care of itself. This is wrong. All of your interviews should stem from a single question:

What would I want to know if I was listening to this interview?

It sounds easier than it is. But a lot of newcomers make the mistake of impersonating other interviewers. They ask the questions they think they should ask instead of asking questions they're actually interested in.

Listen Up

One of the most important interviewing skills is the ability to listen under pressure. Maybe you're taking notes. Maybe the microphones are acting up. Maybe you're fighting off a head cold. No matter what else is going on, you have to be aware of what you and your interview subject are saying.

The last thing you want to do is say something really stupid or, worse yet, gloss over something really compelling the interview subject said. Maybe you're talking to a famous business executive who mentions in passing that they used to clean toilets for a living. Or the singer you're interviewing makes a quip about a former band mate.

Your listeners will be yelling at their speakers if you miss one of these golden opportunities. Amateurs frequently move on to the next question on their list, while pros will say things like:

- "Tell me more about that."
- "What do you make of that?"
- "How did that make you feel?"

The goal is to make your interviews into a conversation instead of a seesaw pattern of question, answer, question, answer, etc. If things are going really well, you may not have a chance to ask any of your prepared questions.

Exercise #6

Imagine you're about to interview your favorite actor, musician or artist. What would you ask them? Make a list of 10 questions or topics you would like to discuss. Be careful not to include questions that can be answered by reading the bio on their official website. Also, try not to ask anything that has been asked in every other interview.

This exercise won't automatically make you into an effective interviewer. That only comes with experience. But focusing on questions that only you can ask will eventually set your work apart from amateurs.

APPENDIX A

EXAMPLE SCRIPT

This example script has been included for reference as a writing sample. Due to the fact that this book is not printed on standard letter-sized paper, the formatting will not appear exactly as described in the preceding chapters.

For a PDF of the following example script, visit www.mikeeiman.com/PodcastScript.

8/1/2017

PODCAST JAMS, EPISODE 1
Written By
Mike Eiman

MUSIC: **PODCAST JAMS INTRO SONG**

ANNCR: Hello, world. I'm Mike. You are listening to Podcast Jams. And we are going to make podcasting easy.

MUSIC: **FADE OUT**

ANNCR: Hey everyone. Welcome to the first official episode of Podcast Jams. This goes along with my recent blog post called "Writing Your Podcast." Head over to PODCAST JAMS DOT COM and click the BLOG tab to check that out.

It's actually an excerpt from my upcoming book about podcasting. Writing scripts. All that good stuff. My book should be ready for release on Amazon Kindle in the next month or so.

Keep an eye out for that.

Anyways. Let's talk about "talking on paper." What's that mean? It means that you don't talk the same way you write.

The writing style we learn in school uses visual cues. Punctuation marks. Paragraph breaks. Headings.

A good writer can pack a lot of information into a sentence. Like the opening to the Charles Dickens' novel OLIVER TWIST. That goes a little something like this:

DICKENS: "Among other public buildings in a certain town, which for many reasons it will be prudent to refrain from mentioning, and to which I will assign no fictitious name, there is one anciently common to most towns, great or small: to wit, a workhouse; and in this workhouse was born; on a day and date which I need not trouble myself to repeat, inasmuch as it can be of no possible consequence to the reader, in this stage of the business at all events; the item of mortality whose name is prefixed to the head of this chapter."

HOST: Dear God. Imagine if you had to talk to someone who sounds like that. You couldn't follow what they're saying. I've got nothing against Dickens, but yikes.

When you're talking, you have to keep things short and simple. There's actually something called a simple sentence. A simple sentence has a subject, a verb and a complete thought.

That means that a person or thing – does something – for some reason.

For example: Bob walked to the store.

Pretty clear. You can use other kinds of sentences that I describe in my blog. But simple sentences are where it's at.

Let's go back to Charles Dickens. What happens if we take that one, long sentence and turn it into simple sentences? Simple language.

Minimal punctuation.

It might sound something like this:

DICKENS: There's a town that I'm not gonna name. One of the many buildings in that town is a workhouse. Oliver Twist was born at this workhouse. The date really doesn't matter.

HOST: Now, if you're a big fan of English literature, you probably can't believe I just did that. If you like clear communication, you might be wondering, "Why didn't Dickens just say that?"

An author might assume the reader will backtrack if they miss something. You can't assume someone's going to rewind your podcast.

Radio listeners don't even have the option. Just assume anyone listening to your podcast is busy. They don't have time to figure out what you're trying to say.

Keep things short and to the point. Look to see if you've got too much punctuation. Break long sentences into two shorter ones.

Instead of saying, "Bob, who was running dangerously low on coffee beans, walked to the grocery store," think simple.

"Bob walked to the store. He was running dangerously low on coffee beans."

Now you know about simple sentences. You're probably an expert by now. What else can you do to write better scripts?

I'll tell you. Two words. Sentence fragments.

You don't always have to use complete sentences. If I asked you, "Do you have any clean spoons?" You might say, "Yes. In the drawer." You wouldn't say, (English accent) "Yes. I have seventeen clean spoons luxuriously aligned in the cupboard drawer located in the main dining quarters." "A" - I already knew we're talking about spoons. And "B" that's way too much information.

Unless I have amnesia. In which case, I forgot. Who are you anyway? Where am I? Why do I need a spoon in the first place?

Are we having ice cream? Cool. Do you have any clean spoons?

Sentence fragments make your speech sound natural. Less formal. Do it.

Tip number two – parenthetical statements.

You see, parenthetical statements are throwaway phrases we use to start a thought. I might say, "Ya know, when I woke up this morning I had a good idea." Then I'd say, "Of course, most of my ideas are good."

"Ya know," "Ya see," "Of course," "I mean." You probably say this stuff all the time. But you don't write it. I'm telling you – write it. Just don't overdo it. Parentheticals make great transitions from idea to the next. Especially when you can't think of a good transition.

Ya know, it's like anything. I mean, you can start every sentence this way. You know, it's not the end of the world. Of course, I'm already sick of hearing myself talk this way.

Case in point.

Tip number three — contractions.

No. You aren't having a baby. Unless you are. In that case, congratulations. Contractions are when you mash two words together. The words CAN and NOT become CAN'T. (Hal 9000) "I'm sorry, Dave. I can't do that."

The words THERE and IS become THERE'S. "There's nothing wrong with this expired bread."

Once again, this is something that works great in speech. Just don't write your master's thesis that way. I repeat. Don't.

Tip number four – emphasis though repetition.

Repeating things gives them a certain authority. A certain – authority.

If I'm talking to you about my friend, Mortimer, it's better to say Mortimer again than to say "him" or "my friend." Especially if I casually mention Carol. Because Carol is another name. You already shifted your focus. And just a few seconds later, you may have already forgotten what my other friend's name was. What was it? Carol and … hmm … Oh yeah! Mortimer. My old pal Mortimer.

Mortimer and Carol. Not him and her.

I hope this has been helpful. I mean, what do I know? I'm an amateur at this stuff. Unfortunately, no one else has compiled a system for writing and preparing a podcast. Seriously, look it up. You can find books and articles that claim to be about writing scripts and outlines.

But the content leaves a lot to be desired. I'm not sure if someone wants to keep this stuff a secret. I don't really know what to think. I feel like I'm reinventing the wheel. Hopefully, my experiments will save you the trouble of having to do the same.

I've wanted to do a podcast for a while now. I finally got tired of trying to find someone to tell me how.

If you have any requests or ideas or vicious and degrading

criticism, please feel free to send it my way.

MUSIC: **FADES IN UNDER VOICE**

ANNCR: My name is Mike Eiman. This is Podcast Jams. And – together – we're going to make podcasting easy.

I've got a bunch of stuff in the works. A lot of great content. Just keep checking back on PODCAST JAMS DOT COM.

Follow us on Twitter AT PODCAST JAMS. Like us on Facebook at FACEBOOK DOT COM SLASH PODCAST JAMS.

Thanks for listening. Let's keep jamming.

MUSIC: **PLAYS UNTIL FADE OUT**

APPENDIX B

SCORING SHEET

How do you know if you're doing a good job? When you're just starting out, you may not have a large following to tell you when you're boring them or doing something really irritating.

That's where it's helpful to be able to critique your own work and decide for yourself if there's something you could be doing better.

Listen back to your recorded podcasts and use the following rubric to assess your performance.

VOICE:

Pleasant ___

Unpleasant ___

Harsh ___

Raspy ___

Throaty ___

Nasal ___

Too high ___

Too low ___

DELIVERY:

Reading ___

Monotone ___

Impersonal ___

Stumbling ___

Too fast ___

Too slow ___

Too loud ___

Too soft ___

ENUNCIATION:

Distinct ___

Mushy ___

Overdone ___

Whistling sibilants ___

Stammer ___

Mispronunciation ___

(Give numerical rating 0-10)

Conversational, friendly ___

Stiff, formal ___

STYLE OF WRITING:

(Give numerical rating 0-10)

Conversational, informal ___

Formal, impersonal ___

SUBJECT MATTER:

Attracts attention ___

Does not attract attention ___

Holds interest ___

Loses interest ___

Gains interest ___

Logical development of subject ___

No apparent organization ___

Strong conclusion ___

Weak conclusion ___

About the Author

Mike Eiman is a lifelong resident of Fresno, CA. He graduated from California State University Fresno in 2010 with a bachelor's degree in theatre arts and a minor in mass communications and journalism.

Mike worked as a journalist for seven years, primarily covering local governments, law enforcement and criminal justice.

You can find Mike on the web by visiting www.MikeEiman.com. Or follow him on social media:

- Facebook: mikeeimanauthor
- Twitter: @mikeeiman
- Instagram: @mikeeiman

Made in the USA
Las Vegas, NV
20 August 2024